PRESENT POETS

Present Poets

Poems for the
Museum of Scotland
compiled by Jenni Calder

NATIONAL MUSEUMS OF SCOTLAND

Published by National Museums of Scotland Publishing,
Chambers Street, Edinburgh EH1 1JF

© Trustees of the National Museums of Scotland and the poets 1998

British Library Cataloguing in Publication Data
A catalogue record of this book is available from the British Library

ISBN 1 901663 14 0

Cover illustration © Lynneke Mulholland
Designed by National Museums of Scotland Publishing
Printed in the United Kingdom by Cambridge University Press,
Printing Division

Present Poets

Contents

Present Poets
giving the past a future

In the spring of 1996 the NMS invited Scotland's foremost poets to write a poem for the new Museum of Scotland. The poems were to be displayed on the hoardings that surrounded the site for the new building going up at the west end of Chambers Street in Edinburgh.

There was an enthusiastic response, and the project expanded into a collaboration with Edinburgh Art College, whose students illustrated the poems, with support from the Scottish Arts Council. The first ten poem posters went up in July 1996, when the project was launched with a general invitation to submit poems. Over 350 poems were received, and from these a selection of a further 40 poems was made by a panel of four: Professor Roderick Watson of Stirling University, Aonghas Macneacail, Gaelic poet, Catherine Lockerbie of *The Scotsman* and Jenni Calder of the NMS. By the time the Museum of Scotland opens, in December 1998, each of these poems will have been displayed on the site hoardings.

Poets were asked to write a short poem on a subject relating to the natural or material evidence of Scottish life and culture. The resulting collection brings together a striking range and variety of poems from many hands - unknown and unpublished as well as experienced and distinguished. It reflects many aspects of Scotland's past and present, and many responses. Some poems directly engage with the role of museums and artefacts in shaping a sense of the past; others explore landscape, people, places, weather and all kinds of activities. A multi-faceted picture emerges, which can be enjoyed for its own sake or read to add a dimension to the experience of the past to be found in the Museum of Scotland.

Among the poems is one of the last written by George Mackay Brown, who, sadly, did not live to see it displayed. The final poem in the collection was not featured on the hoardings, but replaces an extract from one of Robert Burns's epistles, which was displayed to celebrate the bicentenary of his death in 1796.

We would like to express our thanks to the members of the selection panel, to Jonathan Gibbs and his students at Edinburgh Art College, to the designers, printers and joiners who made and installed the posters, and of course to all the poets.

FOR A NEW MUSEUM

We are here to celebrate the marriage
of thought and time. Ignore, please, the rainlike
smirr of footsteps, scutter of a live scarab
hiding. Never mind the steam engine,
the silver spoons, totem pole, the lesser guests.
At the top table let's have true rivets, mighty mastic,
beam and counterthrust, the noble pillars, girders,
oh... Thought has got lost and can't be found
in the crowd. Time spins sunwise, lowps
like a ramstam daftie dancer, stots aff concrete,
jokes wi sandstane. Their bairn's already
born, a house for Scotland's memories again.

Kate Armstrong

ABUIN THEM AA

Gin ae rock conjurs Scotland up for me
It isna Cairngorm quartz, sclenters, scree,
Sanct Giles croon or brig-uphaudin key,
Croon's jasp, cross, or 'stane o destinie',
Nor is it dyke or broch, nor stack nor dun,
Nae fug-clad, rune-scart eemis i' the sun,
Raised beach or sicna prentit fossilry,
Fingal's basalt, pap o Bennachie,
Hud, cairn, whun, sheel, elf-cup, putt or skerry
– The rock that conjurs Scotland up for me
Gies licht in aatum, shines for aa to see,
An' is the hairst Mune, heich an faur an wee.

Colin Donati

GNEISS

Saoilidh mi, nuair a gheibh a' chainnt againn bàs,
Gu bheil e cho coltach ri tachartas,
Gur h-ann fo riasg ann an Eilean Leòdhais
A bhàsaicheas i's a thèid i às,
Na gneiss i's i air a slugadh
Sìos air ais fon talamh
As an do thog i ceann
Na beum aig àm na dìleann.

GNEISS

I suppose, when our speech dies,
That it's as likely as anything
That it'll be in a bog on the island of Lewis
It dies and disappears
As gneiss, sucked back
Down under the ground
From which it first arose
As an eruption at the time of the flood.

Rody Gorman

AGATES

Chateau d'Yquem-coloured, Arran-shaped, terraced
For viniculture, its semi-precious bays
Wait for the never-arriving ornamented boat.
Others are silver, turquoise, red, blue,
Eyes, circles, locked, lapidary vistas
Invented by volcanic accidents.

What draws me to them? Is it words like agate,
Jasp, chalcedony, carnelian, onyx,
Or names of where they came from and can be found? –
Balmerino, Glen Farg, and Scurdie Ness,
Balmeadowside, Iona, and St Cyrus...
Whatever – they are all pieces of universe.

Douglas Dunn

IN THE ROYAL MUSEUM

The blue whale of Portobello
stretches
under the balcony,
its industrial jaws as
tusks turned in
on themselves,
spinal links numbered but
nodding at
limitless range.

Ian Stephen

CARNYX

Priest-mask, pig-snorkel, prow-peak
    glinting in its glass case? Chess-piece
    crafted for Cuchulain; fossil sea-horse
    surfaced from centuries in peat-juice?

Treasure more mysterious: a boar's head
    wrought in bronze; mastery of palate
    and sprung wooden tongue passed down
    in secrecy, Pictish father to son.

Such raucous resonance, from so slender
    a column of air, as struck terror
    into invaders. Fit too to proclaim,
    given occasion, a Nation's resurgence.

Stewart Conn

THE TWEEDSMUIR BOW

to try the draw-weight
   range-finding
to look along the line
   before firing

to shoot the arrow
   make the deer bound
to hear the bow snap
   and fling it down

to go on one knee
   and take away the string
to keep the sinew
   a precious thing

Valerie Gillies

TIME CIRCLES

Mirknen haps a rummelled broch on Houlland's knowe,
rowes hit in a twilt o lavendar: saft smored as a Danish Hjøllund
a year ago. Da line o da prow is sib an da soonds on da tongue,
but dis laand canna scoarn da forest, fat byres and grit rigs o coarn.
Here hit's a tooder o hedder an da mintiest flooers. Fae da broch
da wastside raiks aa aroond: Aid Voe spörs ta da nort, bi wast
a headicraa ta Burrafirt, ta Foula and Waas. Soothbye, a vire o voes
at Sandsoond an Skeld - Skjáldr o da sagas. A year is come
richt roond. I da simmir dim, sungaets, we mark da rim
o da broch-time circles: walk da mairches o a twalmont gien.

Christine De Luca

tooder - tousle
mintiest - tiniest
raiks - roves
spörs - enquires
vire - a great beauty

8

SHANDWICK STONE

As jets without the black box of memory
startle sheep in deserted glens
the stone hunters stalk their various prey.

Chaotic and recurrent as the tides
incised patterns swirl underneath them.
The Pictish beast, that composite

bird-fish-mammal, harbours a smile
having already weathered eras and elements
untraceable by radar.

The rain-clouds gather above an unyielding sea.
Wildflowers and seeding grasses rustle
in anticipation of the next downpour.

Ken Cockburn

ABERLEMNO REVISITED

The standing stone is standing under wraps.
The howe is happed in haar. Pale memories
are ghosts, silently mouthing hieroglyphs.

Seal Tribe. Cat Tribe. The Picts have made their mark.
A coiled serpent, a fish, a roosting bird,
symbolic hand-mirror and double disc

describe an other-ness; a burial chamber
cairn or broch. Listen. Can you hear
the murmurings of their long-dead ancestors?

Turned on its side, this pitted stone takes on
the outline of a whale, its tracery
dissolving in a smirr of acid rain.

Lydia Robb

MAESHOWE

The first island poems
Cuttings in stone
Among the tombs of the very ancient dead,
Young men's lyrics
Struck with chisels among the thronging ghosts
INGIBIORG IS THE LOVLIEST GIRL
HERMUND WITH A HARD AXE CARVED RUNES
A GREAT TREASURE IS BURIED NEARBY
JERUSALEM-FARERS BROKE IN HERE
DRAGON, GUARD THE BONES AND THE VERSES

The young seamen climbed out of Maeshowe,
Their nostrils wide to the salt wind.

George Mackay Brown

RESTORED HOARD

Frae the yird, coggies o siller
that aince were raised tae the lips
o knichts and jarls.

An expert has dichted them
wi muckle care, they skinkle
ahin the gless. Ah canna touch

but ma mind fingers them and feels
biggins alowe, slauchter, and the fear
that gied siller tae the mool.

Donald Adamson

VISIONS

All our land is on loan.
Snow patches recede from Grampian.
Where woodland prances on forgotten paths
a deer-fence journeys over heaths.
Blades and coin wait, rust in buried peat.
The far reaching wind sings fiddlers' tunes.

Mist lifts from an area of dune
and suddenly an ancient shaft
arrowing us, flings down a shard of light
to chance survival, as an outright gift.
Such visions we own.

Sally Evans

LOST VILLAGE

A last few fragmentary belongings -
A brooch, a pendant, a swivel from a dog's lead,
A jug shaped like a man, an ornate padlock
And some arrowheads - all, once, of a township
Lang syne disappeared, buried by the sea and sand.

A last few fragmentary belongings -
A comb, a pan, four cats' heads on a harness clip,
Signs of kiln-sites, broad-edge plough marks
Under the arrowgrass - all, once, of a township
Lang syne disappeared, buried by the sea and sand.

A last few fragmentary belongings.

Colin Donati

THE UISTS

God's fingers left their imprints here;
each loop and whorl
a place for lochs and bays to curl,
spiralling in contours till peaks where
the bone below the moor's laid bare.

And that is why storm-devils come,
peeling back the shoreline till
we clutch on by our fingernails,
knowing soon that all we walk upon
might be stubbed below the ocean's thumb.

Donald S Murray

NAMIN DA PEERIE ISLES

Fae da *Green Holm* scarfs arrow low
mallies bank stiffly troo sea furrows.

Papa, *priest isle*: dere's nane ta lay
haands on, ta sain noo.

Linga, *hedder isle*. A sea hairst:
piltocks, whelks, selkies, waar.

Hildis isle: tree score o sels neebin;
slidder ta safety in Tangi Voe.

Da Shingies: *rocks in sun* at spills gowld.
Tirricks faest, dive low an wild.

Da sels is gien ta Hildasay da day.
Oksna, silent *seal isle*.

Christine De Luca

scarfs - shags
mallies - fulmars
ta sain - to bless
waar - seaweed
tree - three
neebin - dozing
tirricks - arctic tern
sels/selkies -seals

MUSEUM O SCOTLAND

New museum, an al story wrapped in new covers.
Wak through its pages an ye'll fin yer very sel,
a that shaped ye, a that binds ye. Touch
its livin stane, feel history cursin through
yer veins. Listen, it tells us a the same,
wir jist like abody else, but we belang
here. Read well, dinnae rush, but mind o this,
tak it a awa, an Scotland wull still be there.
It bides in the earth, in the very air ye breathe.
Look deep, tak yer time, time is whit this place
is a aboot. Yet, a the while remember,
its no whit ye see, its the way that ye see it.

Derek Ross

MR SCOTLAND

I am embarrassed
By my Kilmarnock bunnet

And brogues; my toorie
And sporran, my umpteen empty quaichs -

What do I really
Have to do with all this,

Carrying my wee boy on my arm?
He intuits that I want to give him everything

But stay shy, though strong enough to know
I am, like you, a drop-dead kist of treasures.

Robert Crawford

BERSERKER
TO A VIKING CHESSMAN

tough tusk,
snuggled in a crushed sift
of limpets gone fine

did you calm in the slack
out of the race, the overfalls,
the politics of navigation?

dug-in, a layer from orchids,
biting your shield,
only from habit

Ian Stephen

THE BONES OF COLUMBA
THE BRECBENNACH

We carry within us the bones of Columba
that carried him into adventure
through the dark age he illumined.

Wise in law, rash in prayer,
peregrinator and protector:
island to island the currents run.

He ploughs our waves of power and war
and harvests scattered tribes of longing
with runes to read, communion bread.

Bones of blessing, *brecbennach*,
at Monymusk, in jewelled casket,
in principle justly among us.

Tessa Ransford

AT THE TOMB OF ROBERT THE BRUCE, DUNFERMLINE ABBEY

In any other country
Your tomb
Would have been worn smooth
By our devotions

But here the notice says:
'Please do not touch.'

They should have left *left* your heart
In Andalucia

Ian Olson

OLD MONASTERY, LOCHABER

How old are these beeches?
Did the 'Heather Monks'
chase deer from their stripling bark?
Did bees fly to the sweet heather
at the back of the sun?

Setting the black beads aside,
did monks lick thick honey
from prayer-blistered fingers?

Tom Bryan

THE TWO

Here there are two chairs
from which the famous two converse.

One wears black, the other red,
and one will be early dead.

One's hair is fair, the other's grey,
one sermonizes all day.

O Bible black, romantic red,
the axe will cut her lovely head.

The sensuous will bow down low
to that cloudy beard as white as snow.

Iain Crichton Smith

PEDEN'S MASK

The mask worn as a disguise by
the Rev Alexander Peden,
Covenanting minister, late 17th century

How, stealing away in the dark,
he would seem too real,
too obvious, like something
pagan, yet going unnoticed, every time:

the stitches of red at the eyes,
the fence-post teeth,
the beard of horsehair, smudged
with fat and blood,

like something mothers use, to scare
their children: one more phantom in the night,
bringing the word of God, that too-smooth face
behind the mask, immaculate as frost.

John Burnside

CROMARTY MAN (c.1837)

Hugh Miller splits another prehistoric page:
Bird tracks like pressed flowers, fish bones
That are diagrams of death, in a book made long
Before his God first thought of him. Miller
Recreates the species, draws lines between them:
No humanoid amphibians crawl from slime,
No blue-arsed Lord Monboddo swings through trees,
Pursued by midwives. But the old coastline beyond
The receded sea rises like the half-dry knowledge
Of his half-drowned fear; and his poised hammer
Is the relic of that pirate ancestor whose ghost
He saw in childhood once, above him on the stair.

James Robertson

TAIRSGEIR

Thairsgeir, chuir mi 'm bogadh thu
aon uair sa' bhliadhna,
deasachadh do chorp
son Mardi Gras na mòintich.
Ach ged a chruthaich thu
na mìltean de dh'fhàdan
a thog mi fhìn
mar dhuan-molaidh dhut sa chruaich,
chaidh do bhàthadh ann an cuan ola
a ghiùlain do spiorad
gu taigh-tasgaidh 'n Dùn Eideann
's a chàraich do chnàimhean a sin.

PEAT-SPADE

Peat-spade, I submerged you
once a year,
preparing your body
for the moorland Mardi Gras.
And although you created
a myriad of peats
which I stacked as a panegyric
on your behalf,
you were drowned in an ocean of oil
which bore your spirit
to a museum in Edinburgh
and there placed your bones.

Murdo Mac Mhurchaidh a Stal

SCOTT MONUMENT

Like Castle Rock
taken for granted,
this stone thing created by hand.

A firtree
or a machine
imagined by Paolozzi?

A rocket
ready for launch
towards some Hibeejambo planet?

A focus
for many postcards
and home for the ghost of a man.

Angus Calder

PLOU SOCK

My faither won prizes for plouin -
   wi steady strides ahent the yoke,
plou sock, worn tae a smooth siller polish,
cuttin clean thro rigs o rich broon earth,
a muckle hearst for pickmaws an peesies.
Single-trees clank in rhythm wi the denty steps
o the Clydesdale. Nae need
for a heavy haun on the rynes,
airm muscles rax tae keep the plou stracht.
Feerin and feenishin deid parallel;
endrigs trig eneuch
for the maist pernickety o judges.

Jean Massie

EAST NEUK

Sleek-backed, rain-black country,
where bramble thorns, like bundles of barbed wire,
tie down the superstitious bones of the long dead.

Their hearts turned in the salt-pans
like nuts; not smoothed or tempered.

Only the knuckles of harbour walls
lay between their whisky warm beds
and the steely sea they fished;
and waves were the voices of scapegoat witches
crying from unplundered tombs.

Wind trawls the cold rinsed coast for the new year,
with its sceptic's face; alert and bony as Fife trees.

Barbara Young

SCRIMSHAW BY A DUNDEE WHALER

He groups his density of dots
like a Daily Record photo. Pokes
with a sailcloth needle, and
in a lonely thought of home
pricks a thumb with the rocking
of the Davis Straits. So blood
will mix with the soot and oil to bring
into sharp relief the lion and the bees
he carves on a Bowhead's tooth. Underneath
he scores the riddle Samson gave them:
'Out of the eater came forth meat;
and from the strong came sweetness.'

Moira Duff

GRUNDSTANE

Thae hauns hae wrocht a lifeline;
wabsters, prenters, lapidars,
watchies, brunties, cairpenters
whase warks cleik wi the heuchsman's
pearls hard howkit fae the mine,
or fisher's fae the watter.
Theirs the cabill we hing tae
sweir tae lowse, for naebody muives
on or he kens whaur he's fae.

Muriel Ferrier

THE MACHINE ROOM

In there the future turned to meet the past.

A child's reach away found pace and motion,
life made vital and intense, involving
all who watched in some conspiracy beyond
the present tense. The power of motors spun
a web of sleight deceit as steam enveloped
mind, imagination and belief. Mines
worked the cages, pistons hissed and spat beneath
the glassy sheen of life. Ships turned the screw
while locomotives led to transports of delight.

In here the future, turned to meet the past,
suspends the present while the motor lasts.

Brian Johnstone

BUTTON TIN

The cheviot and stag lost horny ones when
they headed for the hills. The deciduous trees
left shapely knots when all were gone and
felled. Bloodied, bashed raw iron pins

found trodden in the moor - clasping heather
and mud together when the kilt wasn't safe
to wear. My mother's shell like pearly pair
that winked my father's way, his brassy

army spares that nationally served their day,
duffle coats and quali' dance dresses all
shed them into a tin. I keepsafe my trusted
legacy; history rattles within.

Victoria Husband

RODDY'S MEDAL

He was good at school, a sure high-flier. Here's
the medal in its leather case; silver-gilt
wreathed in fern and daisies *for Excellence
in Classics* 1933 *Tain Royal Academy.*
In 1942 his solo flight fuelled fern and daisies
on a hill not fifty miles from home; his brothers
missing - Willie in the desert, Gregor off to Africa
with bride. They died, the ship sunk, life-boats
strafed in missionary zeal. The telegram that told
the tale was lost, funding further harsh
mythology; for as we wept for one son
drowned in air, newspapers tolled Ocean Tragedy

Anne Macleod

DOMESTIC HERITAGE

A long deal table offers an assortment
of objects - rusty tools, a washboard, spurtles,
paraffin lamps and starched shirt collars, belts -
smelling of dust and mothballs and decay.

These humble relics of our daily lives -
of fashions, skills and techniques superseded -
faded and dented with the passing years,
plunge us headlong into our nation's past.

'D'ye mind yon milk cans that we had tae carry?
An' hoo the kettles was aye black wi' soot?'
A laugh, a sigh; a furtive hand moves out
and strokes the handle of a battered pot.

Mercedes Clarasò

HOPE AND GLORY

Land of soap and soda!
Mother on your knees,
washing stairs and flooring;
bucketfuls and seas

you've sloshed and mopped and carried
across this hall, these stairs.
God who made you humble
may catch you unawares

and on an escalator
raise you to the sun,
where halls of alabaster
need no charring done.

Ken Morrice

MUSEUM CAFE

The three wait.
A bored meeting
of five year olds.

Fingering
sugar crystals,
talking
to the carnation.
They wait
for doughnuts.

Jayne Wilding

ROUSAY TOMB

Miscarried stanes
chockfu o glamorous beads
god-empty submarine
afore Greenock grew.

A sea-way getaway
tae couthier havens.
This yer Scotland, then?
A poke o banes!

John Hudson

A MIDDEN

Grandfather dies. Father dies. Son dies.
We pitch out their worn-out shoes,
The blunt stone tools. Grandmother
Mislays her memory and cannot for the life
Of her remember where the old man buried
The treasure. Mother bites her lip.
And daughter is shaken by terrible tantrums.
We eat berries and shellfish and bits of meat.
White bread, baked beans and Irn bru.
Our descendants shock and astonish us
In equal measure. The family is not jinxed.
It is the natural order of things.

Andrew Wishart

mise, alba

mise, alba, cluaran sporach
dèan tighinn faisg orm   le meatag stàilinn,
ach éisd —

mar a ruith an ceòl thar nan stùc
ann an neòil de chainntearachd
gach lid a glaothaich *mise beatha*

mar a ruith a ghaoth ris a chòrsa fada
linn thar linn
a giùlain a luchd de dh'eòin beag gearanach

a dìon, nam b'urrainn dhaibh, am fearann
mise? alba? cluaran sporach?
nach tig thu stigh, gabh dràm leam

i, scotland

i, scotland, prickly thistle
if you must approach   wear gloves of steel,
but listen —

how the music races over peaks
in clouds of cainntearachd
each syllable crying i am a life

how the wind races on the long coasts
century on century
carrying its cargo of small complaining birds
protecting, if they could, their territory

i? scotland? prickly thistle?
why don't you come in, let's have a dram

Aonghas MacNeacail

40

CEILIDH, GLENUIG

The fiddle sheds resin like sunburnt skin,
cracks head-on with guitar
at a crossroads where Mississippi
clashes with County Clare.
I hear cotton rasping in the rowans.

Piping legends send pibroch to Orion,
fiddlers lift lids from tribal pots,
float slow airs out like birch-leaf boats.

Tom Bryan

EAST NEUK TRIOLET

At Crail, Anstruther, Pittenweem,
the living's lean, the boats are few.
Days are empty as empty creels
at Crail, Anstruther, Pittenweem.
A sighing's in the grey-green sea
as men remember vanished crews.
At Crail, Anstruther, Pittenweem,
the living's lean, the boats are few.

Jim C Wilson

GIVING MEMORY

He gave me memory of my country
Bound in sealskin -
A scattering of pine cones,
A fragment of deer bone,
Granite tempered by the cooling fire
Of long abandoned foundries
Upon which a dead people
Had made their mark.
As he left he apologised
For the piecemeal nature of his gift
But, he explained, he was only a visitor
Just passing through.

Morgan Downie

SCOTLAND'S RAIN

When the rain cleared, the clouds remained as rock
already hardened to an empty landscape, or else
to Georgian buildings and Sixties' slums. Exile's
so familiar that we know the names of every house
and street as if this country were our own.

Listen to the imagined heart we live by,
beating five million lives into
a single life - it is our awakening at last,
to dream of what there was
and what will be when once the rain clears.

Ron Butlin

A ROOMFUL OF MAPS

I'm in a room covered with maps,
And a woman tells me she's going to Australia,
Probably for ever, and I don't see the maps
Till she's stopped talking, and then I see
A map of Australia; and only later I realize
I named the other maps, but none remain;
I can tell you some places there weren't maps of,
Places I've got lost, Ben More, Craig Varr,
Tullich, the moon, and whatever
The country is we go to when we die.

Joy Fuller

ALPHA BETTER CALEDONIA

Armlets and the Ballochmyle brooch in Coffins
Dice with Ewers and a Freedom box.
Golf balls, the Hunterston brooch and Inkstands
Join Jacobite relics, the Key to Lunulas
And more exotic jewellery. The Monymusk reliquary,
Symbol of the Scottish nation, exceeds in worth
Notes promissory, Orbliston ornaments and Pistols.
Quaichs, Relics and Spiral armlets aren't found
In Toolboxes, or Urinals: yet Viking brooches,
Wine goblets and the Yetholm shield
Might have been crafted by Ziegler's forebears
In a nation presented proud to the world.

Richard Love

SCRAN

Prince Cherlie's snotter-dichter
John Knox's draawers
And roustit double-wreistit ae-wye plous.
They'se gar them sweim in gless cages
And feed them on pure air
Tae haud them on spylin.
Whit an affa fowk for junk!
Cairt loads o scran
Nae yiss til man nor baest.
Yit seek the richt angle
And ye'll can get a blenk
O yer ain shadda.

Gavin Sprott

LUCKY BAG

Tattie scones, St Andra's bane, a rod-and-crescent
Pictish stane; a field o whaups, organic neeps,
a poke of Brattisani's chips; a clootie well,
computer bits, an elder o the wee free Kirk;

a golach fi Knoydart, a shalwar-kameez;
Dr Simpson's anaesthetics, zzzzzzz,
a gloup, a clachan, a Broxburn bing,
a giro, a demo, Samye Ling; a ro-ro

in the gloaming, a new-born Kirkcaldy baby-gro;
a Free State, a midden, a chambered cairn:
- yer Scottish lucky-bag, one for each wean;
please form an orderly   rabble.

Kathleen Jamie

CHAMBERS STREET TARDIS

Today: three exhibits with the punch of history.
First, a bone dice, rectangular, twice the length
of a modern dice; fixed for games of chance
on shifty sands or rattling under a plaid at night.
Next, a box, the shape of a tissue pack, man-sized.
Tool-box of a leather worker, making his way
under Orkney's pewter skies. Wood carved,
lovingly, somewhere around 600 to 800 AD,
with the continuous scrolls of eternity.
Last: seventeen peg dolls gaze from coffins,
emptied by body-snatchers: loaded dice of history.

Liz Fincham

A LAMP STILL LIT

They just went out for a moment,
to find themselves or to send
a message, and left the light
shining on all their possessions,
the chairs, the cups, the carpet
shipped from Persia, shells
picked from a beach, photographs
of children dressed for school,
and returned a century on,
the lamp still lit, simple,
familiar but all transformed,
fugitive in a small room.

Jenni Daiches

Other titles available from NMS Publishing

Anthology series

Treasure Islands (Robert Louis Stevenson)	ed Jenni Calder
Scotland's Weather	ed Andrew Martin
Scottish Endings: Writings on Death	ed Andrew Martin
The Thistle at War	ed Helen McCorry

Scottish Life Archive series

To See Oursels	Dorothy I Kidd
Into the Foreground	Leah Leneman
Bairns	Iona McGregor

Scotland's Past in Action series

Farming	Gavin Sprott
Fishing and Whaling	Angus Martin
Spinning and Weaving	Enid Gauldie
Sporting Scotland	John Burnett
Making Cars	Alastair Dodds
Building Railways	James L Wood
Going to Church	Colin MacLean
Going to School	Donald Withrington
Leaving Scotland	Mona McLeod
Feeding Scotland	Catherine Brown
Going on Holiday	Eric Simpson
Scots in Sickness and Health	John Burnett
Going to Bed	Naomi Tarrant
Shipbuilding	James L Wood

Scottish Lives series (forthcoming)

Elsie Inglis	Leah Leneman
Lochiel of the '45	John Gibson

General interest

The Scottish Home	ed Annette Carruthers
Tartan	Hugh Cheape
Precious Cargo: Scots and the China trade	Susan Leiper
The Scenery of Scotland	W J Baird
Collections in Context	Charles D Waterston